Prayers for Catholics

Sister Ann Redig, O.S.F.
Reverend James Toal, O.F.M.

ST. ANTHONY MESSENGER PRESS
Cincinnati, Ohio

ISBN 978-0-8199-0503-1

Published by St. Anthony Messenger Press
28 W. Liberty St.
Cincinnati, OH 45202
www.SAMPBooks.org

Printed on acid-free paper.

08 09 10 11 12   5 4 3 2 1

Contents

Lord,
Make me an instrument of Your Peace.

Where there is hatred, let me sow love;
Where there is injury, pardon;
Where there is doubt, faith;
Where there is despair, hope;
Where there is darkness, light;
Where there is sadness, joy.

O Divine Master, grant that I may not so
* much seek*
To be consoled as to console;
To be understood, as to understand;
To be loved, as to love;
For it is in giving that we receive;
It is in pardoning that we are pardoned; and
It is in dying that we are born to Eternal Life.

—St. Francis of Assisi

Morning
· · · · · Prayers

O eternal and ever-blessed Trinity, Father, Son, and
Holy Spirit, with all the angels and saints, I adore you.
From the bottom of my heart, I thank you for all the
favors and benefits you have bestowed upon me, but
especially for having preserved me during the night,
and for giving me this day to serve you. I wish to live
only for you, for your greater honor and glory and for
the salvation of all people. O God, preserve me this
day from all sin and all occasion of sin. Give me the
grace always to do your will and to please you in all
my actions.

Offering to the Sacred Heart

O Jesus, through the Immaculate Heart of Mary, I
offer you my prayers, works, joys and sufferings of
this day for all the intentions of your Sacred Heart, in
union with the Holy Sacrifice of the Mass throughout
the world, in reparation for my sins, for the intentions
of all our associates, and in particular for the intention
of our Holy Father.

Consecration to Mary

My Queen and my Mother, I give myself entirely to you; and to show my devotion to you, I consecrate to you this day my eyes, my ears, my mouth, my heart, my whole being without reserve. Therefore, good Mother, as I am your own, keep me and guard me. Amen.

To Saint Joseph

O glorious Saint Joseph, father and protector of virgins, faithful guardian, to whose care God entrusted Jesus, innocence itself, and Mary, the Virgin of virgins, I pray and ask you, through Jesus and Mary, preserve my heart free from every sin, keep me pure and innocent, and make me serve Jesus and Mary forever. Amen.

For the Dying

O most merciful Jesus, lover of souls, I pray you by the agony of your most Sacred Heart and by the sorrows of your Immaculate Mother, cleanse by your blood the sinners of the whole world, who are now in their agony, and are to die this day. Amen.

Heart of Jesus, have mercy on the dying.

For a Good Heart

O dearest Jesus, whose amiable Heart excludes not even the greatest sinners, when they turn to you, grant, I beg you, to me and to all penitent sinners, a heart like yours:

A humble heart, which, even in the midst of temporal honors, loves a life little esteemed by humans. A meek heart, which bears with everyone, and seeks to be revenged upon no one. A patient heart, which is resigned in adversity and happy even in the most trying circumstances. A peaceful heart, which is always at peace with others and with itself. A disinterested heart, which is always contented with what it has.

A heart that loves prayer and prays often and cheerfully. A heart whose only desire is that God may be known, honored, and loved by all creatures, which grieves for nothing except when God is offended.

A pure heart, which in all things seeks God alone and desires only to please God. A grateful heart, which acknowledges and esteems the benefits of God. A strong heart, which is daunted by no evil, but bears all adversities for the love of God. A heart, liberal to the poor and compassionate toward the suffering. A well-ordered heart, whose joys, sorrows, and desires, whose every motion is regulated according to the divine will.

(St. Clement M. Hofbauer)

For Holiness

Dear Jesus, help me to spread your fragrance everywhere. Flood my soul with your spirit and life. Penetrate and possess my whole being so utterly that all my life may be only a radiance of yours. Shine through me and be so in me that every person I come in contact with may feel your Presence in my soul. Let them look up and see no longer me but only Jesus.

(Cardinal Newman)

NIGHT
· · · · · PRAYERS

O my God, most Holy Trinity, I adore you with all the angels and saints that surround the throne of your infinite Majesty. I thank you, heavenly Father, for having created me; I thank you, Divine Son, for having redeemed me; I thank you, Holy Spirit, for having sanctified me, and called me to your Holy Catholic Church, and particularly for all the graces and favors you have bestowed upon me this day.

Join me, you blessed spirits, in thanking the God of mercies, who is so bountiful to so unworthy a creature.

Come, Holy Spirit, and enlighten my mind that I may clearly see all the sins I have committed this day in thought, word, and action, and give me the grace to obtain full pardon of them by an act of sincere contrition.

Here examine your conscience and then make a good act of contrition

O my God, I am sorry for all my sins because they displease you, who are all good and deserving of all my love. With your help I will sin no more.

Let us pray.

Visit, we ask you, O Lord, this habitation, and drive from it all the snares of the enemy. Let your holy angels dwell here to preserve us in peace, and may your blessing be upon us forever; through Christ, our Lord, Amen.

Bless, O Lord, the repose I am going to take, in order to renew my strength, that I may be able better to serve you. All you saints and angels, the Mother of our God, and dear Saint Joseph intercede for me this night and during the rest of my life, but especially at the hour of my death. May the divine assistance remain always with us.

My Jesus, have mercy on all those who will die this night and grant them eternal salvation.

The Memorare

Remember, O most gracious Virgin Mary, that never was it known that anyone who fled to your protection, implored your help, and sought your intercession was left unaided. Inspired with this confidence, I fly unto you, O Virgin of virgins, my Mother! To you I come, sinful and sorrowful. O Mother of the Word Incarnate, despise not my petitions, but in your mercy hear and answer me. Amen.

SACRAMENT OF
· · · · · RECONCILIATION

The follower of Christ approaching the sacrament of Reconciliation comes with an inner conversion of heart embracing sorrow for sin and intent to lead a new life.

Contrition:
Through carefully examining your conscience with regard to the virtues, the Beatitudes, the commandments and the works of mercy, you come to heartfelt sorrow.

Confession:
Confess your sins, in particular all grave sins, to the priest humbly and frankly.

Penance:
Perform acts of penance and reparation for the sins committed as a renewal of life.

Absolution:
Through absolution by the priest, God grants you pardon.

Begin with a prayer to the Holy Spirit:

Come, Holy Spirit, enlighten my mind that I may clearly see all my sins. Let me not be deceived by self-love, but show me the true state of my conscience. Move my will to sincere sorrow and help me to make a good confession. Holy Mother of God, intercede for me that I may obtain the pardon of my sins. Holy Guardian Angel, pray for me that I may mend my ways.

Examine your conscience:

The Ten Commandments

I.   I, the Lord, am your God. You shall not have other gods besides me.

II. You shall not take the name of the Lord, your God, in vain.

III. Remember to keep holy the Lord's day.

IV. Honor your father and your mother.

V.   You shall not kill.

VI. You shall not commit adultery.

VII. You shall not steal.

VIII. You shall not bear false witness against your neighbor.

IX. You shall not covet your neighbor's wife.

X.   You shall not covet your neighbor's goods.

The Great Commandment:
You shall love the Lord your God with your whole
   heart, with your whole soul, and with all your mind.
You shall love your neighbor as yourself.

The Beatitudes

Blessed are the poor in spirit, for theirs is the
   kingdom of heaven.
Blessed are the meek, for they shall possess the
   earth.
Blessed are they who mourn, for they shall be
   comforted.
Blessed are they who hunger and thirst for justice, for
   they shall be satisfied.
Blessed are the merciful, for they shall obtain mercy.
Blessed are the clean of heart, for they shall see God.
Blessed are the peacemakers, for they shall be called
   children of God.
Blessed are they who suffer persecution for justice's
   sake, for theirs is the kingdom of heaven.

The Theological Virtues
Faith
Hope
Charity

The Cardinal (Moral) Virtues
Prudence
Justice
Temperance
Fortitude

Spiritual Works of Mercy
Counsel the doubtful.
Instruct the ignorant.
Admonish the sinner.
Comfort the sorrowful.
Forgive injuries.
Bear wrongs patiently.
Pray for the living and the dead.

Corporal Works of Mercy
Feed the hungry.
Give drink to the thirsty.
Clothe the naked.
Shelter the homeless.
Visit the sick.

Visit the imprisoned.
Bury the dead.

If you have any difficulty with your examination of conscience or your confession, simply ask the priest for help.

Contrition
After finding out your sins, make an act of real sorrow for them. Your are sorry when you wish you had not committed them and are determined not to do so again. Arouse sentiments of true sorrow. Then say with fervor:

An Act of Contrition
O my God, I am heartily sorry for having offended you, and I detest all my sins because I dread the loss of heaven and the pains of hell, but most of all because they offend you, my God, who are all good and deserving of all my love. I firmly resolve with the help of your grace, to confess my sins, to do penance, and to amend my life. Amen.

After Confession

I give you thanks, O Lord Jesus, because you have cleansed me from my sins. I adore and praise your infinite mercy. I consecrate myself entirely to your love and service. Give me, good God, the grace to avoid sin and the occasion of sin. Mary, my Mother, bless my good resolution, and may the angels help me to keep it.

Holy
 · · · · · Communion

Before Communion

Our Lord in the Holy Eucharist is the divine physician. He can heal both soul and body. Invite him to come often.

The Eucharistic fast has been simplified. You are required to abstain from food and drink for one hour. You may take medicines whenever they are prescribed. Water does not break the Eucharistic fast. If for any reason you are not able to observe these regulations, do not hesitate to talk to the priest or chaplain.

For the sick who cannot be present at Holy Mass, a good way to prepare for Holy Communion is to attend "spiritually." Say some of the following prayers from the Mass for the sick:

Introductory Rites

Be gracious to me, O LORD, for I am languishing;

 O LORD, heal me, for my bones are shaking with terror. (Psalm 6:2)

The Kyrie

Lord, have mercy.
Christ, have mercy.
Lord, have mercy.

Opening Prayer

Let us pray.
O almighty and everlasting God, eternal salvation of those who believe, hear our prayers. We implore your merciful help for your ailing servants. Restore them to health that they may return thanks to you in the midst of your church. Through Jesus Christ, your Son, our Lord, who lives and reigns with you in the unity of the Holy Spirit, God, forever and ever. Amen.

Reading I

Are any among you suffering? They should pray. Are any cheerful? They should sing songs of praise. Are any among you sick? They should call for the elders of the church and have them pray over them, anointing them with oil in the name of the Lord. The prayer of faith will save the sick, and the Lord will raise them up; and anyone who has committed sins will be forgiven. Therefore confess your sins to one another, so that you may be healed. (James 5:13–16)

Responsorial Psalm

Be gracious to me, O LORD, for I am languishing;
O LORD, heal me, for my bones are shaking with
terror. (Psalms 6:2)

Alleluia, alleluia.

Hear my prayer, O LORD;
   let my cry come to you. (Psalm 102:1)

Alleluia.

Gospel

When he entered Capernaum, a centurion came to
him, appealing to him and saying, "Lord, my servant
is lying at home paralyzed, in terrible distress." And
he said to him, "I will come and cure him." The
centurion answered, "Lord, I am not worthy to have
you come under my roof; but only speak the word,
and my servant will be healed. For I also am a man
under authority, with soldiers under me; and I say to
one, 'Go,' and he goes, and to another, 'Come,' and
he comes, and to my slave, 'Do this,' and the slave
does it." When Jesus heard him, he was amazed and
said to those who followed him, "Truly I tell you, in no
one in Israel have I found such faith. I tell you, many
will come from east and west and will eat with

Abraham and Isaac and Jacob in the kingdom of heaven, while the heirs of the kingdom will be thrown into the outer darkness, where there will be weeping and gnashing of teeth." And to the centurion Jesus said, "Go; let it be done for you according to your faith." And the servant was healed in that hour.

Prayer Over the Gifts

O God, by your will the span of our lives is measured. Accept the prayers and offerings of your servants on behalf of the sick for whom we implore your mercy. May we, who now fear for their safety, soon rejoice in their restoration to health. Through Jesus Christ, your Son, our Lord, who lives and reigns with you in the unity of the Holy Spirit, God, forever and ever. Amen.

Preface

All-powerful and ever-living God, we do well always and everywhere to give you thanks through Jesus Christ our Lord.

At the Last Supper, as he sat at table with his apostles, he offered himself to you as the spotless lamb, the acceptable gift that gives you perfect praise. Christ has given us this memorial of his passion to bring us its saving power until the end of time.

In this great sacrament you feed your people and strengthen them in holiness, so that the family of humankind may come to walk in the light of one faith, in one communion of love.

We come then to this wonderful sacrament to be fed at your table and grow into the likeness of the Risen Christ.

Earth unites with heaven to sing the new song of creation as we adore and praise you forever.

Holy, Holy

Holy, holy, holy, Lord God of power and might. Heaven and earth are full of your glory. Hosanna in the highest. Blessed is he who comes in the name of the Lord. Hosanna in the highest.

Eucharistic Prayer

In memory of his death and resurrection we offer you, Father, this life-giving bread, this saving cup.

We thank you for counting us worthy to stand in your presence and serve you.
May all of us who share in the body and blood of Christ be brought together in unity by the Holy Spirit.

Lord, remember your church throughout the world; make us grow in love.

Remember our brothers and sisters who have gone to their rest in the hope of rising again; bring them and all the departed into the light of your presence.

Have mercy on us all; make us worthy to share eternal life with Mary, the Virgin Mother of God, with the apostles, and with all the saints who have done your will throughout the ages. May we praise you in union with them, and give you glory.

Conclusion

Through him, and with him and in him, in the unity of the Holy Spirit, all glory and honor is yours, almighty father, forever and ever. Amen.

The Lord's Prayer

Let us pray.

Taught by the Savior's command and formed by the word of God, we dare to say: Our Father, you are in heaven, holy be your name; your kingdom come; your will be done on earth as it is in heaven. Give us this day our daily bread; and forgive us our trespasses as we forgive those who trespass against us; and lead us not into temptation, but deliver us from evil.

Deliver us, Lord, from every evil, and grant us peace in our day. In your mercy, keep us free from sin and protect us from all anxiety as we wait in joyful hope for the coming of our Savior, Jesus Christ.

Lord Jesus Christ, you said to your apostles: I leave you peace, my peace I give you. Look not on our sins, but on the faith of your church, and grant us the peace and unity of your kingdom where you live forever and ever. Amen.

The Agnus Dei

Lamb of God, you take away the sins of the world, have mercy on us.

Lamb of God, you take away the sins of the world, have mercy on us.

Lamb of God, you take away the sins of the world, grant us peace.

Communion of the Sick

The priest shows the Holy Eucharist to the sick person and says: This is the Lamb of God who takes away the sins of the world. Happy are those who are called to his supper.

The sick person joins the priest in saying: Lord, I am not worthy that you should come under my roof. Speak but the word, and my soul will be healed.

Priest: The Body of Christ

Response: Amen.

Let us pray.

O Lord, Holy Father, almighty and eternal God, trustfully we beg of you that the most sacred Body of your Son, our Lord, may be a lasting remedy of both body and soul for our (brother/sister) who has just received it. Amen.

Communion Antiphon

Do not let me be put to shame, O LORD,
  for I call on you;

...

Let your face shine upon your servant;
  save me in your steadfast love. (Psalm 31:17, 16)

The Prayer After Communion

Let us pray.

God our Father, our help in human weakness, show
our sick brothers and sisters the power of your loving
care. In your kindness make them well and restore
them to your church. We ask this through Christ our
Lord. Amen.

After Communion

*After Communion, spend some time in fervent prayer
and thanksgiving. The following prayers, as well as
the prayers on pages 4 and 44, may be of help to
stimulate your own warm response to Christ who has
just come to you. Let your heart speak.*

SPECIAL
• • • • • PRAYERS

Act of Love

O Jesus, how shall I return you thanks for the goodness in giving yourself to me? The only way I can repay your love is by loving you in return. I love you, and I desire to love you all my life.

Jesus, you alone are sufficient for me. Whom shall I love, if I love not you, my Jesus? You love those who love you. I love you. Oh, do you also love me? If I love you but little, give me the love which you require of me. O Mary, my good Mother, and you, glorious Saint Joseph, lend me your love to love Jesus.

Act of Offering

O my divine Lord, I offer you my body and its sense, my soul and its faculties, my heart and its sentiments. My thoughts, my desires, my words, my actions, my whole being are yours. Since you have given yourself wholly to me, can I do less than give myself wholly to you? Grant me, O divine Jesus, to persevere in your holy love. Give me a still greater sorrow for my past sins, and strengthen the sincere resolution I have formed never again to offend you.

For a Happy Death

O my Lord and Savior support me in my last hour in the strong arms of your sacraments and by the fresh fragrance of your consolations. Let the absolving words be said over me, and the holy oil sign and seal me; and let your own Body and Blood be my food. And let my sweet Mother, Mary, breathe on me, and my angel whisper peace to me, and my glorious saints and my own dear patrons smile upon me, that, in them all and through them all, I may receive the gift of perseverance, and die as I desire to live, in your faith, in your church, in your service, and in your love

(Cardinal Newman)

To Christ Our King

Christ Jesus, I acknowledge you to be the King of the universe. All that has been made is created for you. Exercise over me all your sovereign rights. I hereby renew the promises of my baptism, renouncing Satan and all Satan's works and pomps; and I engage myself to lead henceforth a truly Christian life. And in a special manner do I undertake to bring about the triumph of the rights of God and your church, so far as in me lies. Divine Heart of Jesus, I offer you my poor actions to obtain the acknowledgment by every heart of your sacred kingly power. May the kingdom of your peace be firmly established throughout all the earth. Amen.

Anima Christi

Soul of Christ, sanctify me; body of Christ save me; blood of Christ, inebriate me; water from the side of Christ, wash me; passion of Christ, strengthen me; O good Jesus, hear me; within your sacred wounds hide me; permit me not to be separated from you; from the malignant enemy, defend me; in the hour of my death call me; and bid me come to you, that with your saints I may praise you forever and ever. Amen.

Prayer Before a Crucifix

Look down upon me, good and gentle Jesus, while before your face I humbly kneel, and with burning soul pray and beseech you to fix deep in my heart lively sentiments of faith, hope, and charity, of true contrition for my sins, and a firm purpose of amendment; while I contemplate with great love and tender pity your five wounds, pondering over them within me, while I call to mind the words which David, your prophet, said of you, my Jesus: "They pierced my hands and feet / I can count all my bones."

(Psalm 22:16–17, *NAB*)

Act of Resignation

O Lord, my God, from this day I accept from your hand willingly and with submission, the kind of death that it may please you to send me, with all its sorrows, pains and anguish.

Spiritual Communion

I believe that you, O Jesus, are in the most Holy Sacrament. I love you and desire you. Come into my heart. I embrace you. Oh, never leave me. May the burning and most sweet power of your love, O lord Jesus Christ, I beseech you, absorb my mind that I may die through love of your love, as you were graciously pleased to die through love of my love.

(Saint Francis)

To the Sacred Heart

Most sweet Jesus, Redeemer of the human race, look down upon me. I am yours and yours I wish to be; but to be more surely united with you, I freely consecrate myself today to your most Sacred Heart. Be King, O Lord, not only of the faithful who have never forsaken you, but also of the prodigal children who have abandoned you; grant that they may quickly return to their Father's house, lest they die of wretchedness and hunger. Be king of those who are deceived by erroneous opinions or whom discord keeps aloof, and call them back to the harbor of truth and unity of faith, so that soon there may be but one flock and one shepherd.

Grant, O Lord, to your church assurance of freedom and immunity from harm; give peace and order to all nations, and make the earth resound from pole to pole with one cry: Praise to the divine heart that wrought our salvation; to it be glory and honor forever. Amen.

To Our Blessed Mother

Mary, Mother of God, graciously hear our prayers, and receive our petitions, which we united with those of all the faithful on earth and of the angels and saints in heaven. Intercede for us, most loving Mother, and obtain for us the greatest of all graces—to be faithful to you and to your Son, unto death, and after death, to obtain the happiness in heaven of praising, blessing, and thanking you, with all the angels and saints, and with you, love and honor your beloved Son, Jesus Christ, together with the Father and the Holy Spirit, through all eternity. Amen.

COMMON
· · · · · PRAYERS

In the name of the Father, and of the Son, and of the Holy Spirit. Amen.

Our Father, you are in heaven, holy be your name; your kingdom come; your will be done on earth as it is in heaven. Give us this day our daily bread; and forgive us our trespasses as we forgive those who trespass against us; and lead us not into temptation, but deliver us from evil. Amen.

Hail Mary, full of grace! The Lord is with you; blessed are you among women, and blessed is the fruit of your womb, Jesus. Holy Mary, Mother of God, pray for us sinners, now and at the hour of our death. Amen.

Glory be to the Father and to the Son, and to the Holy Spirit. As it was in the beginning is now, and ever shall be, world without end. Amen.

The Apostles' Creed

I believe in God, the Father Almighty, Creator of heaven and earth; and in Jesus Christ, God's only Son, our Lord, who was conceived by the Holy Spirit, born of the Virgin Mary, suffered under Pontius Pilate, was crucified, died, and was buried. He descended into hell; the third day he arose again from the dead; he ascended into heaven, sits at the right hand of God, the Father Almighty; from there he shall come to judge the living and the dead. I believe in the Holy Spirit, the Holy Catholic Church, the communion of saints, the forgiveness of sins, the resurrection of the body, and life everlasting. Amen.

Act of Faith

O my God, I firmly believe that you are one God in three Divine Persons, Father, Son, and Holy Spirit. I believe that your Divine son became human, and died for our sins, and that he will come to judge the living and the dead. I believe these and all the truths that the Holy Catholic Church teaches, because you have revealed them, who can neither deceive nor be deceived.

Act of Hope

O my God, relying on your almighty power and infinite mercy and promises, I hope to obtain pardon of my sins, the help of your grace, and life everlasting, through the merits of Jesus Christ, my Lord and Redeemer.

Act of Love

O my God, I love you above all things, with my whole heart and soul, because you are all-good and worthy of all love. I love my neighbor as myself for the love of you. I forgive all who have injured me, and ask pardon of all whom I have injured.

Act of Contrition

O my God, I am heartily sorry for having offended you, and I detest all my sins, because of your just punishments, but most of all because they offend you, my God, who are all-good and deserving of all my love. I firmly resolve, with the help of your grace, to sin no more and to avoid the near occasion of sin.

The Angelus

V. The angel of the Lord declared unto Mary.

R. And she conceived of the Holy Spirit. Hail Mary, etc.

V. Behold the handmaid of the Lord.

R. Be it done unto me according to your world. Hail Mary, etc.

V. And the Word was made flesh.

R. And dwelt among us. Hail Mary, etc.

V. Pray for us, O Holy Mother of God.

R. That we may be made worthy of the promises of Christ.

Let us pray.

Pour forth, we beseech you, O lord, your grace into our hearts, that we to whom the incarnation of Christ, your Son, was made known by the message of an angel, may by his passion and cross be brought to the glory of his resurrection, the same Christ our Lord. Amen.

To My Guardian Angel

Angel of God, my Guardian dear, to whom God's love commits me here, ever this day be at my side, to light and guard, to rule and guide. Amen.

Before Meals

Bless us, O Lord, and these your gifts, which we are about to receive from your bounty, through Christ our Lord, Amen.

After Meals

We give you thanks for all your benefits, O Almighty God, who lives and reigns forever; and may the souls of the faithful departed, through the mercy of God, rest in peace. Amen.

On Entering or Leaving Church

We adore you, O Christ, and we bless you, here and in all the churches of the whole world, because by your Holy Cross you have redeemed the world.

SACRAMENT OF THE ANOINTING OF · · · · · THE SICK

This sacrament is for all who are sick. It should normally be celebrated in the presence of the sick person's relatives and friends, who actively participate. It consists of the laying on of hands by the priest, the prayer of faith and the anointing of the sick with oil, conferring grace.

Anointing the sick person with oil on the forehead and hands, the priest prays: Through this holy anointing may the Lord in love and mercy help you with the grace of the Holy Spirit. May the Lord who frees you from sin save you and raise you up. Amen.

Let us pray.

Lord Jesus Christ, you shared in our human nature to heal the sick and save all humankind. Mercifully listen to our prayers for the physical and spiritual health of our sick (brother/sister) whom we have anointed in your name.

THE WAY OF
· · · · · THE CROSS

Sick people and others legitimately impeded can make the Way of the Cross by reflecting on each station:

Jesus is condemned to death.
Jesus bears his cross.
Jesus falls the first time.
Jesus meets his mother.
Simon of Cyrene helps Jesus carry his cross.
Veronica wipes the face of Jesus.
Jesus falls a second time.
Jesus meets the women of Jerusalem.
Jesus falls a third time.
Jesus is stripped of his garments.
Jesus is nailed to the cross.
Jesus dies on the cross.
Jesus is taken down from the cross.
Jesus is placed in the tomb.

THE
• • • • • ROSARY

The rosary is the prayer most pleasing to our blessed
Lady. Although the complete rosary consists of
twenty decades, we usually mean five decades when
we speak of the rosary.

To Pray the Rosary

Begin with the Sign of the Cross, say the Apostles'
Creed, the Our Father, and three Hail Marys for an
increase of faith, hope, and charity, and a Glory be to
the Father. Then say the Our Father, ten Hail Marys
and one Glory be to the Father for each of the five
decades. While saying these prayers, try to picture to
yourself the various scenes of our Lord's life, as they
are recalled in the mysteries.

The Joyful Mysteries

The Annunciation
The Visitation
The Nativity
The Presentation
The Finding in the Temple

The Sorrowful Mysteries
The Agony in the Garden
The Scourging
The Crowning with Thorns
The Carrying of the Cross
The Crucifixion

The Glorious Mysteries
The Resurrection
The Ascension
The Descent of the Holy Spirit
The Assumption
The Coronation

The Luminous Mysteries
(The Mysteries of Light)
The Baptism of the Lord
Jesus' Self-Revelation at Cana
Jesus Preaches the Kingdom of God
The Transfiguration
The Institution of the Eucharist

OTHER
· · · · · PRAYERS

In Time of Sickness

Jesus, Our Lord, we ask you to have mercy on all of us who are sick. Give us your strength and love, and help us carry this cross with faith. May our sufferings overcome the power of evil and lead others to our Father in heaven.

Lord Jesus, hear our prayer, for you are our Lord forever and ever. Amen.

For the Chronically Ill

Loving Father, have mercy on those who suffer from constant sickness or weakness. Give them the courage to share with Jesus in carrying their cross for the salvation of the world.

Reward their faithful love by peace now and by eternal happiness and joy in heaven.

Father, we ask this prayer through Christ our Lord. Amen.

In Time of Sickness and Trial

O good Jesus, I accept willingly this sickness (or trial) which it has pleased you to lay upon me. I confide all my pains to your Sacred Heart, and beg you to unite them with your bitter sufferings and thus perfect them by making them your own.

Lord Jesus, our God, have pity on us who suffer for love of you. Help us to carry our cross each day with you, and to share with you in saving the world. Give us courage and strength, and a share in your glory, for you are Lord forever and ever. Amen.

Before Surgery

Lord Jesus, help us as we prepare for this operation. In your love, guard and protect us. Through the skills of the doctors and the care of everyone, bring us back to health and full activity. Lord Jesus, we praise you forever and ever. Amen.

After Surgery

Loving Father, we give you all praise and glory for your merciful love. We thank you for granting us a safe recovery, and we ask you to continue to protect us. Father, we ask this blessing through Jesus Christ our Lord in the love of your Holy Spirit, one God, forever and ever. Amen.

Come, Holy Spirit

Come, Holy Spirit, fill the hearts of your faithful and enkindle in them the fire of your love.

V. Send forth your spirit and they shall be created.
R. And you shall renew the face of the earth.

Let us pray.

O God, who by the light of the Holy Spirit, did instruct the hearts of your faithful, grant that by that same Holy Spirit, we may be truly wise, and ever rejoice in your consolation. Through Christ our Lord. Amen.

My Breastplate

Christ be with me, Christ within me, Christ behind me, Christ before me, Christ beside me, Christ to win me, Christ to comfort and restore me, Christ beneath me, Christ above me, Christ in quiet, Christ in danger, Christ in hearts of all that love me, Christ in mouth of friend and stranger.

(Saint Patrick)

A Prayer of Self-Offering

Lord, I freely yield all my liberty to you. Take my memory, my intellect and my entire will. You have given me all that I am and all that I have; I give it all back to you to stand under your will alone. Your love and your grace are enough for me; I shall ask for nothing more.

(Saint Ignatius Loyola)